Qoheleth

William F. DeVault

Copyright © 2024 Venetian Spider Press™
& William F. DeVault
All rights reserved.
ISBN-13: 9798989048113

To the Word

Annunciation 1

Poetry of Qoheleth 9

   Incandesce 11

   The Duty of Poets 12

   wisdom 13

   passion 13

   The living forge 14

   perceptions 15

   All is vanity 16

   The transcendent 17

   there is no Hell 18

   Resonance 19

   Scriptures 20

   blood or mud or ink on flesh or memory 21

   Karma 22

   Redemption and Fall and Rise 23

God is not within you 24

chitin 25

nothing but artifice 26

finding the word within 27

facets 28

the essence of metaphors 29

word is consecration and revelation 30

the justice of the word 31

respect the muse 32

honing the edge of sanity 33

presence in solitude 34

the spectrum of life 35

finding creation 36

the sermon 37

the nature of the word 38

The Words of Qoheleth *41*

Flesh in the Abattoir *45*

To acknowledge/Credits *53*

William F. DeVault

Annunciation

Qoheleth

Do not be deceived, even by your own sense and senses.

It was not light nor matter nor energy that first announced the universe...it was a word.

The word of the omniscient, eternal poet that uttered existence onto the blank page of time and all dimensions.

There is just one poet, one poetry, one expression, viewed in different moods and lights and angles and prejudices, seeming sometimes as a multitude, or as a trinity, or as a dispassionate unity.

But there is only one.

There is truth to be taught. And learned.

I am Qoheleth, a teacher. A splinter of the truth.

Qoheleth

Beyond scripture, beyond the voice of the speaker, beyond the limitations of any language or of all languages, even that of music and light.

For a common comprehension, we shall call it poetry.

Every time you read these words you will understand a little more. Your mind, your spirit, permitting greater comprehension without breaking you. For a broken vessels holds nothing of value, nothing of virtue. But still has value and purpose.

You are limited by your perceptions and the impressions and metaphors you draw from those perceptions. There are things that existed before you were born, before anyone was born. But they existed, nonetheless.

Love existed before you drew breath. Before you were aware of yourself, of your mother, of touch and warmth. There are corners of existence you will never see, never know, that you lack even the subtext to imagine.

But they exist. All those things existed.

William F. DeVault

Thus did the Poet exist.

There is poetry in every insect or bird that flies.

Every tear or drop of blood shed. In the orbits of the planets around infinite suns in infinite galaxies.

But the Poet is not insignificant. The Poet is like gravity, universal, if often subtle.

The spirit is within us. It is within everything. You do not need to see or feel it to realize it, to attune your mind and soul to it, for it does not need your permission or acknowledgement to exist.

Ignorance is unto itself, it does not make something more or less real. Truth is truth.

Let us be true to all things.

We, as mortals. think and reason in the simplest of frames.

Three dimensions. Four in rare moments. As our minds can hold such a small piece of the ultimate truths.

Qoheleth

Yahweh acknowledges that "the word" began it all.

Who would understand this better than poets? Poets are ultimately the priests, the prophets. Ecclesiastics.

We serve, whether we are brave enough to admit it or not, one or more or all of the faces of God. For all are splinters of the tree of life and the fabric of existence, sentient beyond out most limited awareness of sentience.

We are not the children of Qoheleth. We are, when speaking truth, Qoheleth.

We seek and speak truth beyond the façade, beyond the dimensions of mortal observance.

The children of infinite mothers and fathers, our blood is a pretense. A vessel that carries the words.

The Word.

Poetry is a sacred outreach to others of the revelation of God, or a prayer to God. It is truth.

William F. DeVault

Love, peace, hope. Essential. But if not based in truth and expressed in poetry, mere vanity.
We are all part of a greater webwork of mortal intelligence and awareness, which are not one and the same.

I could describe a simple stone ten thousand ways, based on colour or shape or size, taste, scent, the texture or sound it makes when struck.

So it is with God.

There are not 3 or twelve or 100,000 deities.

Just one, experienced and perceived in different ways by different people at different times in history and in different lights and emotional states and stakes.

There are more ways to perceive God than there are flower petals in an endless meadow, more than different snowflakes in a glacier, more than there are stars in the sky.

God is not male or female, merely labelled as such by those requiring something common to hold onto.

Qoheleth

There is nothing wrong with perceiving a fragment of God, as long as your perception does not bring you to fear or hate or regard as wrong others who encountered God in a different light or time or from a different angle.

The faith and practice is founded on self-examination and awareness of the natural world.

There is no supernatural world, only those elements of the natural world we have not perceived, or having perceived, have not understood or accepted.

The poetry of the universe is far more than one mind can grasp, we can only perceive and reveal small facets.

All are poets. But just as both sand and boulder are both rock, there are greater and lesser poets and poems.

The poet is not the essential, the atomic, expression, but it is the poem that defies us as the poem celebrates the universe.

In the poem we find and express truths, both receiving from the universe, from God, as well as expressing, speaking to, God and the universe.

William F. DeVault

Poetry of Qoheleth

Qoheleth

William F. DeVault

Incandesce

by the light of a single candle
the night is pressed away.
not too far or for too long.
the dawn shall finish it off.
but, in its turn, only temporarily.
we are each tapers waiting our turn
to burn and dance with unique fire,
driving away the darkness, fighting
fear, doubt, and lighting the way
for those who will, in turn, follow.

Qoheleth

The Duty of Poets

Truth is the absolute. The responsibility
to the past, the present, and the future.
We see with eyes and
hear with ears and
taste with tongues
blessed to experience things mundane and mystical.
To deny what is observed, what is revealed,
in disregard of the duty of poets.
to trivialize that which is fundamental and
universal and
revelation of the divine.
The supernatural does not exist.
All is natural.
All is truth.
The duty of the Qoheleth.

William F. DeVault

wisdom

poets are the prophets
poets are the priests
poets set the sabbaths, the holy days, the feasts

naught is supernatural
nothing is obscured
the veil is our perceptions, wisdom is secured.

passion

stones struck to make a spark in dark hollows
that last only an instant, or catch the karma kindling
to illuminate and warm us, form us from ores
of past or pretense, advancing the evolution
of hearts and minds in perfected kinds
that drip the very fluids of life.

the Word is spoken or merely internally chanted
and incanted as a spell that seeks to control
our hearts and parts moved to motive creation
in retrospect and to perfect the dance of decades.

Qoheleth

The living forge

In the shadows and silence
he bleeds and he breeds,
the seeds and sediments of his prison
a prism that distorts his vision,
shifting the spectrum.
prism, a prison, a schism bound in
cuir bouilli and sweat-wetted silk.
a liaison of the three parts, the quintessence
through which the tachyons scream
to redeem the darkest reaches unpenanced.
I burn him with light and logic,
tempting him with the padparadscha
and the blistered moissanite forged
in my furnaces under Mount Aetna.
he is my life force when Aphrodite is not present.
the blood of Bragi lubricates my instruments, shackled
to words and mortal frame.
bartering immortality for passion.
and the reverse.

William F. DeVault

perceptions

It is essential to note that every stone,
be it pebble or boulder,
is made of much the same thing.
It I merely a question of magnitude.
Thoughts and feelings,
whether grounded in truth
or merely perceptions
are much the same,
all that varies is their granularity,
similar weight.

The poet, the lover, the parent, the child,
none create an obligation
by their existence or nature.
The dream does not own the dreamer.
Likewise, the dreamer does not own the dream
as they pass through the veil of revelation.
We are by our natures, selfish creatures,
separated by want and need from the truth
that the word, the poem, the poet,
would exist without us.
We are as lenses to the light.

Qoheleth

All is vanity

Be silent.
Beyond utterance or thought.
Finding the essence of time and existence.

You were not here yesterday
and will not be tomorrow
and all your joy and sorrow
will not even be memory in the stream
of life others contemplate
unless expressed with clarity and passion.

William F. DeVault

The transcendent

The universe is a living thing.
Sentient beyond imagining.
Phillips said your God is too small.
He was right.
The universe is a living thing.
The way it defines
good and evil...
we cannot judge, but trust the virtues of life,
seeking light in the darkest corners
of this all-encompassing whole we inhabit.
Arrogant
enough to insist that the consciousness
must conform to the virtues we command it to,
our prayers are not spells.
We do not command the transcendent
with our whims.
Ungrateful for our existence and our harvest
of love and life.

Qoheleth

there is no Hell

Mythologies are not truth but the comfort of liars.
Since ancient times we have buried our dead
and from time to time when volcanoes (or such)
reveal what is deep in the ground, we speak of
a lake of fire as where those who do not accelerate
into the infinite universe, abide in agony.
We are not born with souls, with true consciousness,
but are granted by the Transcendent upon transit
from the world of flesh to truly join the universe.
If granted, by whatever criteria is required,
we sweep out on winds faster than light to leave
the flesh behind, to find liberation, consecration
in the infinite body of the universe.
The Transcendent does not wish a damning pain
on those not born a second time when the chrysalis
breaks open and we are graduate to the dance.
The dance on winds brighter than stars.

William F. DeVault

Resonance

All perception, all perceptions and perspectives,
meaningless
unless the sound or
vision or
touch or
taste or
scent
resonates with us, within us,
allowing us to grip the slippery surfaces
of reality and make a connection to what we already
know or think we know.
The lessons of light and life and Word
must find resonance within us
the universality of
the romance of
the wisdom of
the purpose of
the poetry
that exists and existed before there was a word for it.
That will exist when the final embers
of stars yet unborn
flicker and die.

Qoheleth

Scriptures

Every word, written or unwritten,
in memory sustained or lost to the winds
that blow cold from the hearts of the unrepentant,
is scripture in the ethereal book of time.
Just as pain is proof of life, the call to rise
often misunderstood as a command to stay down
beneath the weight of exhaustion and suffering,
so is joy the bite of tiny animalcules whipping you
to be aware of the fleeting instants of time
in which the perfect moments are presented
as respite from suffering and sorrow.
Celebrate all as too soon the opportunity
to worship and rejoice is lost in darkness
where only the echoes remain and sustain.
The Word transcends time and space and places
both suffering and hope in our hands
to drink as water in the parching sun.

William F. DeVault

blood or mud or ink on flesh or memory

record. remember.
set the taut strings vibrating with new thoughts
caught on the hot fibers and sinews, true to new
and old recollections from before
and after
laughter at the funeral
when apropos.
Kairos over Chronos.
eggs hatch and stone cracks bones
as we atone for what we thought and said and did.
for all things we utter or conceive or enact
are facts in the tapestry, threads and beds and heads
thwarted and consorted as we transport dreams
from preconscious to conscious to incantations
that penetrate the wind and stone and light
with or without our willful expressions.

Qoheleth

Karma

Fate and destiny based on the balance.
Madness or manipulation.
Seeking order in the chaos that is the true
nature of the universe, the necessity
of mythology to reassure us
that pandemonium is not our proving ground
for we are children needing reassurance
that all things work for us because we
are more significant than the universe
and the truth offends our brittle egos.
Abused by the powers-that-be to compel
obedience to papier-mache artifice
to accept the fabrication,
the making sense of the dice
of the natural order of a quantum universe.

William F. DeVault

Redemption and Fall and Rise

We are who
we are.
Frail. Failed. Brittle bitter souls,
hollowed out by pain and loss.
No one is irredeemable.
Penance is the path,
for we must forgive ourselves
that we may think and reason clearly.
To unburden our hearts.
The world weighs us all down.
All of us have our darkness and our
splintered edges that dredge the light
to scuff rough edges but does not pledge
our allegiances to foul tempers.
All swords must endure the flame, some shatter
and scatter in fragments,
others take temper and glow in the night.
Bright as sunrise.

Qoheleth

God is not within you

I. God is not within you. You are within God. God is not thrown down by your prejudices. Your lies. Your fervent scrambles to justify all manner of evil. War and the sores of the shores of, lies we tell the world because the truth frightens us. We are not the center of the universe. Eppur si muove.

II. God is not within you. You are within God. The stench of our own native flaws bends laws that we cannot break as we take snake-in-Eden pride in our deceptions. Labels before definitions. Definitions before truth. The proof that what we are and what we say has validity, obscured by our cowardices.

William F. DeVault

chitin

we must turn ourselves inside out.
bring our vulnerable selves to the surface.
capture the chitin to our very cores
that we may feel, in truth and raw sensation,
but when the deepest cuts burn our souls
our cores deflect the killing blows
for it is in pain that we find life.
for it is in life that we find pain.
weep if you can, scream if you must,
unleash your words and revelations
as undoubtably the start of creation
was pulled in agony from nothingness,
for creation, birth, is a violent act
with searing sorrow, pain, and words.

Qoheleth

nothing but artifice

we are born, live, and die in uncertain times.
others will tell you what they believe and
what you should reconcile to your existence.
strangely, they seek validation in your faith.
truth does not bend to belief. prayers and
recitations are not the word, but words,
glitter against the sunrise, providing nothing
but artifice.   nothing but comfort against
real pain and the encroaching darkness,
sparks but no flame, momentary flashes
with no sustained illumination.
speak to what you see, perceptions
and perspectives expressed that all may
gain advantage from our revelations.
in the beginning was the word
but our words advance the proposition
of our awareness and understanding.

William F. DeVault

finding the word within

seek silence and speak from a place of truth
that you along have known, intimate in a manner
that you recognize the voice that whispers,
glass and black sands, fires fanned with breath
that counts the steps along the way.

eloquence and insight, light brighter than memory
in retrospect we genuflect to protect our earnest
inheritance, to know the difference between
good and evil, and have the courage to rise
and walk the shifting, drifting path.

the word, the words, are not in the wind,
but within you. sacred truths, vespers of more
than just life, but the very strands of reality,
speaking like cithara strings strummed and plucked
to invoke the dance of the decades.

Qoheleth

facets

even the most seemingly perfect of spheres
is made up of planes and lines and facets
that are often imperceptible unless you gaze
directly into these compound eyes of the word.
you must accept this, embrace this, just as
you accept invisible truths in the science
of understanding life and experience, smooth
surfaces upon intense scrutiny become rough
and rugged and so surprisingly not what
we thought on first glance.

William F. DeVault

the essence of metaphors

we and all we perceive, if only marginally,
can only be understood in metaphors.
red is only red when compared to perceptions
in paint and fruit and lips and blood,
likewise, darkness and light, pain and delight,
interpreted by what we express and confess
and what those who read or hear our words
know or have known in past experience,
expressions and subtle or blatant words
that carry the resonance to communicate
love and hate, pictures we relate,
to invoke, provoke, in ink and spoken word.

Qoheleth

word is consecration and revelation

holy of holies, the Word is in the rain
and the desert
and the airless expanse of space
where there is beauty in the desolation.
brittle and bitter, the aspects of elephants
being burned into the idols of Babylon.
we confess and bless, lifeless stone,
molten metals, adorned with gemstones
and the bones of our ancestors, crushed
and made into powders and paints
to adorn worshippers and the fallen
as our guttural cultures demand and remand
to the mysteries of histories and glyphs.
symbols and sigils and words cut into flesh,
willing and unwilling, to denote ownership
or dedication, tattoos of lusts and crusts
of scars never sealed, never healed or concealed.
that we may speak and interpret by our petty
prejudices and wisdom, mythologies and religions
made from the inference engines of our real
and artificial intelligences, as history permits.

William F. DeVault

the justice of the word

justice is not revenge
an eye for an eye
a tooth for a tooth
that is balance in the maddest
of scales
where only blood washes blood
where only pain compensates pain
it is a lie that feeds our most primitive
our most ignorant lies and sides
justice is cold for heat
healing for pain
comfort for sorrow
life for death
it is difficult, but true
it is arrogant and wrong
to poison the future for the past
to cast stones against the memories
and sustain the evil of anger
there is righteous indignation
but it should not feed ignorant action
we should seek to be better
to rise above our worst instincts

Qoheleth

respect the muse

whatever you desire and that inspires you,
draw strength and an understanding of life
as your words flow into and from the word
as an act of sacred awakening and joy.
respect the muse
protect, and choose
to adorn the heavens
and your heart with beauty and hope.
a pen is barren without inspiration.
do not denigrate what fills you
with emotions and dreams
with words and eloquences
amomancies beyond flesh
that embrace great and trace
essences of experience
and observation and prayer.
for every poem is a prayer
whether shouted to the masses
or whispered as a lover's vesper
as echoes, then fades,
but invades in the moment
it is conceived and revealed.
respect the muse
for even the instant is sacred.

William F. DeVault

honing the edge of sanity

not every sacrifice is worthy.

the edge. the point. the mettle of the metal
must prove itself suitable to pierce the silence
with resounding presence and power, flowers
bursting from the soil made ready for life.

the sand, the dust, that you are laboring in
may prove unfit to bear leaf, then blossom,
then fruit to evidence the effortless labors
that feed the universe and universal life.

hone the edge, prepare the way for emergence
of refractions and reflections of inspiration.
do not mock the miracle of the word.
do not forget your obligation for your gifts.

not every sacrifice is worthy.

Qoheleth

presence in solitude

seek an unique solitude. answerable only
only
only
to your own voice. which is the voice within.
captured in the silence with deafening chaos
that resolves to a symphony of magnitudes
screaming a thousand entreaties, concurrent
until you rend the woven tapestry of time
and tempest, wresting threads thinner
than the most elegant superstrings
and pluck these, the tension tearing flesh
until your fingers bleed and your tongue
tastes the tempest and the tedium again
again
again
and only once. glyphs resolving to words.
words only you hear, as you are
the only one listening
and capturing the prayers of the faithless
the lost
the living
that will listen. if not today, then one day.
and bless you for your efforts.

William F. DeVault

the spectrum of life

no sentient life is perfect in intent and action.
there are always impurities, even if preconscious,
complexities and vexities that confound reason
and reasons we have lost in the haze and fog.
likewise, there is no perfect darkness, for purpose
is an evolution, a battered blend of ingredients
whipped together until we have no ability
to explain our every nuance, our every whim.

life is a spectrum. more colors than you can count
and every flash shifts in wavelength and intensity,
for there is no perfect white or black or red
as the shades parade and the hues fight
for not just dominance, but inclusion, to be
at least a trace in the infinite composition
that those who listen closely enough can discern
an elegant harmony and counterpoint, if subtle.

Qoheleth

finding creation

in all things, seek the creation, the echoes
of the word that birthed everything
that you may observe and comprehend
what has been brought forth, begging
the acceptance of the dancing dreams
that surround and confound rationale.
this is the light and shadows, the miracle
that we can only celebrate and mimic
in our own thoughts and words, our hearts
enlightened and made aware of the essence
that we are part and prophet of, finding
the nature of life and thought, caught
on and in the web of the superstrings,
slick and sticky building fabrics that weave
all beauty and terror of what has passed
and what we will see if we turn eyes
to the elegant horizons yet to come.

William F. DeVault

the sermon

we are all, part and of the whole, the children
of the word and the words, casting our prayers
against the earth and sky, to live, to die, to try
to find the revelation we revel in, awakened
to catch raindrops on parched tongues, thirst
that is quenched when drenched with the truth.

make earnest offerings to the eyes and ears
of a profoundly pregnant universe folded myriad ways
into dimensions and representations of life and love,
the building blocks of all reality, the words burning
to lay a kiss of memory and forgetfulness
drawing breath from the night and filling hope.

bear witness and speak truthfully and passionately,
revealing what we have seen, heard, felt, and learned
from the texture of the transubstantiation, thoughts
made word made real to seal us into our tombs
of celebratory sentiences, delighting in the light
as we paint our presences on the tapestries of night.

Qoheleth

the nature of the word

neither and both, female and male, beyond
simple binary reasoning, portrayed as the writers
have sought to depict and define it, often
for simple minds, seeking a basic reassurance
that what remains within our definitions.

but the word is not something you can grasp
by just labels and the play of concepts, glib
slogans and appearances, icons of manipulations
that make sport and contort the reality
which is far mor beautiful than our limitations.

language cannot capture it, for it birthed the tongues
of Babylon, Shubur, Hamazi, Sumer, Uri-ki, Martu,
and all others, as many as there are and have been
variations on the simplest of truths, that language
communicates and yet confounds or thoughts.

the word does not need the puffery of artifice
but bears itself in the words of the poets,
the Qoheleth, the Amomancers, the silent dancers
that tell their tales in earnest hips and lips
honeyed like a sad-eyed Rahab, whispers and shouts.

William F. DeVault

the nurture of all nature is found in the continuity
found in the words of the bearers of the word,
barefoot and arrogant, or humble and downcast,
unsilenced by the violence of indifference of those
ignorant and unwilling to split to vent the springs.

Qoheleth both learn and teach, assembling those
who have the humility to listen when they speak
with the tongues of angels in eloquence, understood
for the words must be of common revelation
that they are not just the clutter and clatter of drums.

fingertips in sand or clay, ink in pens, electronic
glyphs and capture, bodily fluids on lover's flesh,
expressions that open the veil for a higher form
of commune, war against isolation and ignorance,
loneliness expressed physically and intellectually.

no word is profane. nothing unnatural, supernatural,
for the order of the universe is an expression
of the word and all the variations that sprout
to wither or bloom in kind and time, leaving
traces to feed future thoughts and recitations.

Qoheleth

the nurture of all: it one is found in the continuity
found in the words of the bearers of the word,
barefoot and arrogant, or humble and downcast,
unsilenced by the violence of indifference of those
ignorant and unwilling to split to vent the sponge.

Qoheleth both loans and teach, assembling those
who have the humility to listen when they speak
with the outrageous of angels in eloquence, understood
for the words come be of common revelation
that the parts come part of shibbor and shatter or shatter.

flagrants in some reaches, as in prose, electuary,
glyphs and copious. Fleshly builds all lover's flesh,
expressions that open the self out chatter form
of commune, wordless interlocution and opinion of
loneliness expressed singularity and unfellowship.

no word is prologue to lasting unheard, all a word
for theories of the universe is an expression
of the word and of the vehicles of a sprout
no wither of blood it in kind and more flashing
traces to feed future thought and retribution.

40

William F. DeVault

The Words of Qoheleth

Qoheleth

William F. DeVault

Be moderate in all things, except that what you are truly passionate about. Let history judge you by your passions.

As we all see, hear, taste, smell, and feel things as different, so are our perceptions of the Word. Our experiences and our lessons have reinforced our perceptions but still we do not perceive the totality of the infinite.

All religions and belief systems are shards of the stained glass. No mortal mind can comprehend the entire vision of the infinite consciousness that is the Word.

A whim is not a thought, a thought is not an action, an action is not more than a solitary wave in the ether, the current must be caught and amplified.

A quote is just a tattoo on the tongue.

Shouting a lie does not make it true.

Qoheleth

The opinion of an atheist does not disprove the existence of God.

The opinion of a believer does not prove the existence of God.

All muses are revelations and worthy of respect and awe, that which drives us to communicate with and of the Word is wondrous.

To be a poet is to be Qoheleth, a teacher and a pilgrim, Searching for and revealing the infinite truths bound in the Word as it is revealed to us. Our poetry must be more than glossolalia, more than gibberish produced when our minds and souls are overwhelmed. It is an Holy purpose and we must seek to be worthy of it.

William F. DeVault

Flesh in the Abattoir

Qoheleth

Anyone can "read a poem". Sitting or standing. To themselves or to one or more other people.

In whispers like vespers or even via a microphone. But to READ a poem that was written by yourself, publicly, is another level of presentation.

To me poetry is not just pretty words, but a snapshot of the deepest depths of the soul, the making of oneself truly vulnerable, self-immolation.

I have compared it in the past to presenting one's heart and soul, as earnestly as possible, to a prospective lover, in the presence of hostile kin and strangers, who are armed.

To do justice to a poem, having the integrity of the artform, we must be that committed and passionate about it.

First, let's be fair, most people will never find themselves in either situation.

Qoheleth

Most people do not write poetry. If they read it or the works of others in public it is for classwork or the like, and they have no flesh in the abattoir, so to speak.

They mumble, making no eye contact, often not even comprehending what they are saying. The gravity of a dust mote, not that of a magnetar.

The stage fright they may feel is shallow, not that of a martyr who is weeping their amomancy with a fierce couer rage that bids to rip their living heart out and incinerate it.

We must consider the intensity of the work, even if it cleverly hides the truth behind the words, behind the intent of the author.

Perhaps this is why, however expertly, we can discount well-performed readings of works we ourselves have not authored, for there is a true intimacy in
poetry, a truth that transcends craft and style and school, only the author can truly know the quintessence.
Whether the words represent the birth of a universal notion or the wasting death of an heroic virtue, they must carry power of a grand scale.

William F. DeVault

In the beginning was the word, so says the King James Version of The Holy Bible, equating "word" and God, it is only when we embrace the power and magnitude of the words that we are worthy of poetry.

I am credited with thousands of works, millions of words, and it is only when I leave myself behind that I feel worthy of my creation.

And then to have to utter the words to one or to many, that is swallowing again the divine airs I have already released.

It is terrifying, it is euphoric, it is stripping the most intimate elements of myself naked and offering my flesh and blood as new communion to those who may be indifferent or even hostile to the sacrifice.

The dreams of the damned, the tears of the willing sacrifice.

Passion, in all the meanings of the word, is what matters.
There are those, poets and prophets, who have been flayed alive for merely being earnest, for speaking with an understanding of what they are saying.

Qoheleth

If you are not willing to express great truths, even in the minute details (even "I love you") then you are not READING POETRY.

Those who wrote and write great poetry leave bloodstains on the altars to their deities.

Do not defile their memories with platitudinous shadow puppets against the background radiation of the echoes of the big bang.

Get your flesh in the abattoir.

William F. DeVault

Qoheleth

To acknowledge/Credits

It is difficult to write, honestly and with clear conscience, and acknowledgement to those who have inspired and guided me, intentionally or inadvertently. Often against the very rationale for their words and actions.

So, I won't, beyond to say many, many have influenced and awakened me, in part. I love you all, even those who have done what they did for cruel or selfish or misguided purposes. I have been honored by your truths, disappointed in your deceptions, wounded by untruths told to me, but worst of all about me.

To those who had the difficult task of reviewing this document without judgement, without having me burnt at the stake or declared a heretic. Or worse.

I have written what I have out of earnest expression, to purge and pacify that within me not defiled by the darkness that I have seen.

Qoheleth

Flesh in the abattoir was previously published in *Harbinger Asylum's farewell edition: series one* under the eye of the legendary Dustin Pickering.

William F. DeVault

Qoheleth

Milton Keynes UK
Ingram Content Group UK Ltd.
UKHW042306010724
444881UK00002B/3